YOU CAN DRAW
FAIRIES
AND PRINCESSES

by Brenda Sexton

PICTURE WINDOW BOOKS
a capstone imprint

MATERIALS

Before you start your amazing drawings, there are a few things you'll need.

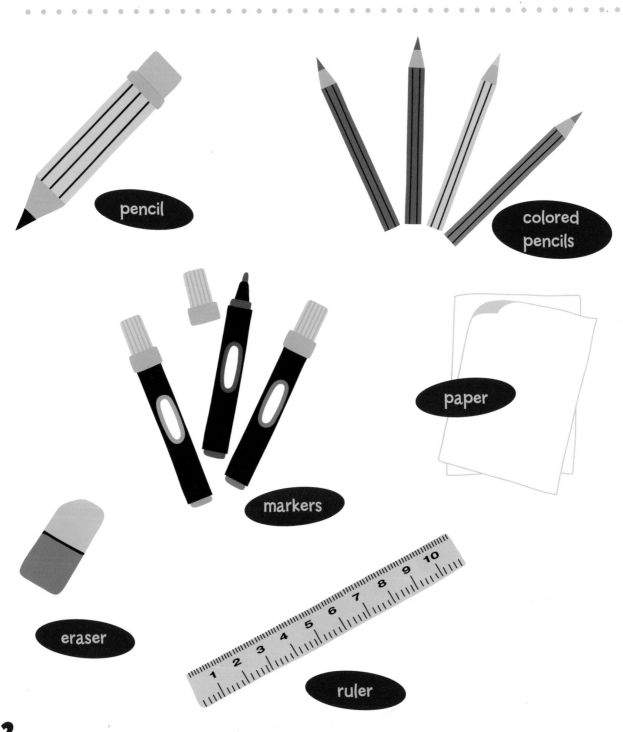

pencil

colored pencils

markers

paper

eraser

ruler

SHAPES

Drawing can be easy! In fact, if you can draw these simple letters, numbers, shapes, and lines, YOU CAN DRAW anything in this book.

letters

DSLU
VZ

numbers

123

shapes

lines

CUPCAKE FAIRY

WARRIOR PRINCESS

1.

2.

3.

4.

5.

6.

7.

8.

9.

10.

11.

12.

5

FUTURISTIC PRINCESS

1.

2.

3.

4.

5.

6.

7.

8.

9.

10.

11.

12.

BUTTERFLY FAIRY

1.

2.

3.

4.

5.

6.

7.

8.

9.

10.

11.

12.

PIRATE PRINCESS

1.

2.

3.

4.

5.

6.

7.

8.

9.

10.

11.

12.

Now try this!

8

BUMBLEBEE FAIRY

1.

2.

3.

4.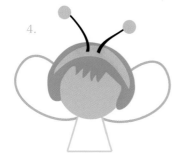

5.

6.

7.

8.

9.

10.

11.

12.

STARDUST FAIRY

1.

2.

3.

4.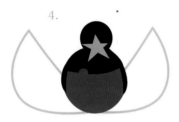

5.

6.

7.

8.

9.

10.

11.

12.

ICE PRINCESS

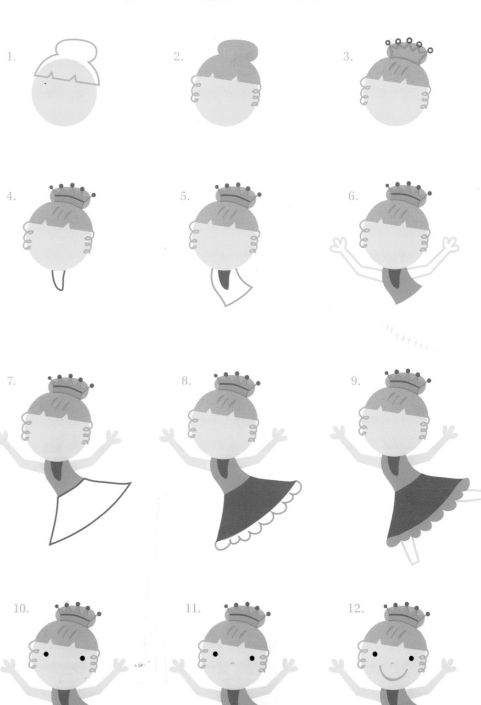

EGYPTIAN PRINCESS

1.

2.

3.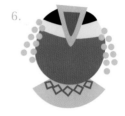

4.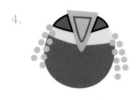

5.

6.

7.

8.

9.

10.

11.

12.

RAINBOW FAIRY

1.

2.

3.

4.

5.

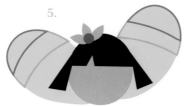

6.

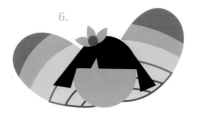

7.

8.

9.

10.

11.

12.

13

NIGHTMARE FAIRY

1.

2.

3.

4.

5.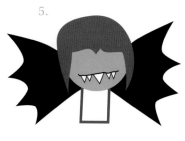

6.

7.

8.

9.

10.

11.

12.

ALIEN PRINCESS

CANDY PRINCESS

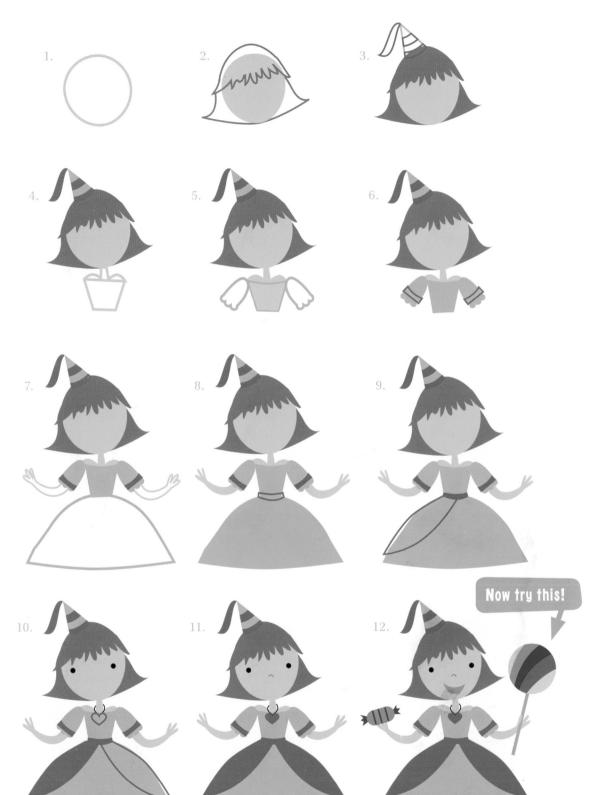

Now try this!

TOOTH FAIRY

1.

2.

3.

4.

5.

6.

7.

8.

9.

10.

11.

12.

17

BOOK FAIRY

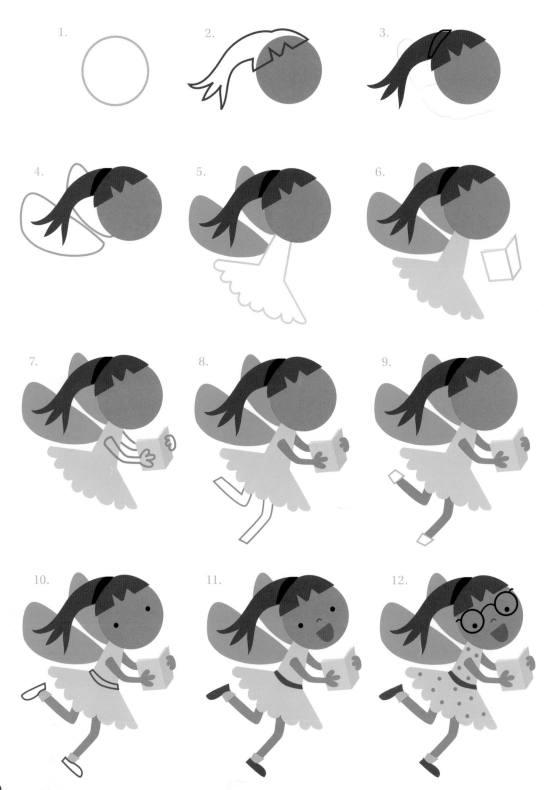

EVIL PRINCESS

1.

2.

3.

4.

5.

6.

7.

8.

9.

10.

11.

12.

TEACUP

BIRD

TOOTHBRUSH

VASE

SILVERWARE

TEAPOT

GINGERBREAD MAN

CAKE

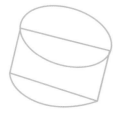   

21

All books published by Picture Window Books are manufactured with paper containing at least 10 percent post-consumer waste.

Library of Congress Cataloging-in-Publication Data
Sexton, Brenda.
  You can draw fairies and princesses / by Brenda Sexton.
    p. cm. — (You can draw)
  ISBN 978-1-4048-6808-3 (library binding)
  1. Fairies in art—Juvenile literature. 2. Princesses in art—Juvenile literature. 3. Drawing—Technique—Juvenile literature. I. Title. II. Series.

NC825.F22S49 2012
743.4'4—dc22   2011006997

Printed in the United States of America in North Mankato, Minnesota.
032011   006110CGF11

Picture Window Books
151 Good Counsel Drive
P.O. Box 669
Mankato, MN 56002-0669
877-845-8392
www.capstonepub.com

Editor: Shelly Lyons
Designer: Matt Bruning
Art Director: Nathan Gassman
Production Specialist: Sarah Bennett
The illustrations in this book were created digitally.

Internet Sites •

FactHound offers a safe, fun way to find Internet sites related to this book. All of the sites on FactHound have been researched by our staff.

Here's all you do:

Visit *www.facthound.com*

Type in this code: 9781404868083

 Check out projects, games and lots more at
www.capstonekids.com

Look for all the books in the **You Can Draw** series: